LISTEN TO MY

STORY

❡

migration_miteinander e.V

A Collection of Dynamic Stories & Interviews

Bibliografische Information der Deutschen Nationalbibliothek: Die Deutsche Nationalbibliothek verzeichnet diese Publikation in der Deutschen Nationalbibliografie; detaillierte bibliografische Daten sind im Internet über dnb.dnb.de abrufbar.

© 2019 by migration_miteinander e.V.

Herstellung und Verlag: BoD – Books on Demand, Norderstedt

ISBN: 9783750423343

CONTENTS

Preface

Chapter 1: Education & Training

Chapter 2: Mobility

Chapter 3: Identity & Family

PREFACE

This book is a collection of stories from young people who share a desire to have their inner voices heard. The gathering of these stories was motivated by our strong desire to spread love and help establish inclusion and foster the spirit of *'ubuntu'* in our society through storytelling. *'Ubuntu'* is a Nguni word meaning, having qualities that include the indispensable human merits; compassion and humanity. This can be achieved by taking young people with and without a refugee background on equal terms and have them share their stories with the rest of the world and build lessons from that.

In the past few years, our world has faced a great wave of migration, and this has caused a great deal of controversy in our diverse societies. No one is willing to listen or answer questions regarding the reason why our world is in this situation. These questions include why do people move, why are they coming into our societies for safety, what will happen to our society? The stories were all gathered from testimonies and personal interviews and they intend to be the answer to those mystic questions. The book might seem to be a little flare of light in gross darkness, but it has the power to lead our society to a brighter and integral society!

Most of the stories in this book were gathered from person- al interviews and are written in third person narrative. There is, however, exceptions and those were written in first person narrative since the stories came directly from the individuals. All of the stories in this book have proved beyond doubt to be factual and great care was taken to avoid misrepresenting the reader.

The book is organized into 3 chapters:
Chapter 1: Education & Tradition
Chapter 2: Mobility
Chapter 3: Identity & Family

migration_miteinander

✼

CHAPTER 1

EDUCATION & TRADITION

"Education empowers people"

Benjamin is a 22-year old student, born in Germany born studying in Italy. Travelling is helping him understand and learn more about other cultures. Benjamin believes that one can learn through travelling; to him travelling is a form of education. From his educational experiences, Benjamin is now able to scientifically define the term education.

"My teacher for social pedagogy told me that the definition of education is in the word. Education as a word comes from Latin; 'e' means to pull, to pull the best out of a person and this is what I think education means." As a Social and cultural education student in Bologna, Benjamin spends most of his time doing voluntary work. During his voluntary stints, he is able to gain knowledge of different cultures. Volunteering has helped him gain experience in interacting with people from different cultural, educational and social classes.

Benjamin believes that one can educate himself through music and dance. Picking a reference from one of the youth exchanges that was organized by migration_ miteinander, Benjamin said that he learnt a lot from the music and dance moves that were showcased by participants from different nationalities. "I educate myself with music a lot. Since different cultures have different rhythms, for example in this project now (referring to the (Y)our Europe Youth Exchange) we have a lot of participants who are from the Middle-East and their musical approach is very different and their music is immediately recognizable; you can immediately associate it to their region," he explained.

Benjamin explained how music and dance holds a special place in the Middle-East and the same standard cannot be said of Germany and he is ashamed of the fact that he is German, but he doesn't know 'German dances'. "It's super interesting to see how music is important to them (referring to people from the Middle-East). They all know the lyrics, they all know the sounds, and they all know some cultural dances as well. Me, for instance, from Germany, I don't know my traditional dances and it's not such a 'cool thing'."

Benjamin (right) conversing with another participant during the (Y)our Europe Youth Exchange Program. (Photo: migra- tion_miteinander)

For Benjamin, Italian education has shaped him into the young man he is today. He is now able to draw parallels between Italian and German education systems to the effect that he feels less pressured by the Italian education system. To him, educational systems around the world reflect the cultural values of their respective countries.

For one to succeed in life the role of a mentor or role model is important. Benjamin believes that people who have been around him played an important role in shaping him and as a young man he is trying to copy from them. "Every person that has a different point of view on life is educating me when it comes to life," he said.

Education is a process that starts in the family; Benjamin believes that he is very privileged to have parents who gave him what he calls "cultural personal education". When we were young, we always complained about our parents being "harsh" on us when they imposed certain rules and standards. Benjamin considers this process important and can be considered as a form of education.

"When you grow up you understand the educational intention of what your parents did to you. They loved you and I consider myself very privileged because my parents gave me a lot of education; cultural personal education". Education has diversified over the years and new learning methods are being incorporated into the system. Benjamin believed that education and diversity cannot be separated. "I see them (education and diversity) very connected and contemplatory to each other." Separating the two can result in the loss of some aspects in the whole learning process. For education to be diversified there is a need to have new cultures added to our ways of life. When education is not diversified, "right wing tendencies" start to creep in, Benjamin argued stating that when "right wing tendencies" sweep in people start to "close up" and shun diversity.

Story written from an interview with Benjamin Breitwieser (Germany)

4

A Little Girl Who Was Abused When She Left Her Country

*T*his little girl was 8 years old. She fled her country because of war. Syria was in a bad condition.

One day, in a bomb explosion, she lost her father and her brother. Now, she was alone with her mother. Her mother knew they needed to get out of the country. Her only choice was to live with her husband's brother. He was not married. They all lived together until they could get out of Syria.

During this time, the mother and the uncle were in a relationship but the little girl did not know about the relationship. When her daughter was asleep, she went to the uncle's room.

One night, the little girl woke up and wanted some water. She heard shouting and she went near her uncle's room. She opened the door and she saw that he had a stick and he was beating her mother. Her clothes were torn and she was crying.

Suddenly, the uncle was pretending that he was kind to the woman. And the mother told her it was just a game, she was fine. "When we are finished with our game, I will come to your room and sleep with you," she said.

The little girl went back to her room, but she didn't sleep. She was scared; she was thinking of her mother and waiting for her to come. She felt like her mother needed help, but she couldn't say it.

She waited and the mother did not come. Early in the morning she saw her mother leave her uncle's *room and quickly went to her own room.*

It was a holiday and the little girl did not go to school. But everyone else forgot she was at home. She stayed in her room and observed from the window.

After 10 minutes her mother went outside and started to clean the yard. The uncle started calling for the woman to make breakfast for him.

Suddenly, the man who would bring them out of the country called and told the mother they were ready to go. She was happy but the uncle was not happy. He tried to find a way to stop the woman from leaving and stay with him.

In the evening they were waiting for the girl to come home from school, but instead she came out of her room. The uncle told the mother, "If you don't let me have your daughter I will not let you get out of here." Suddenly when the girl heard this she understood this was not a game. She shouted at him and said, "What kind of human are you? You are using our situation. We need someone to protect us."

But the mother agreed with his demand. She apologized and said, "She is small. She doesn't know about these things. We will do what you want; just let us go out of here. I don't want to lose my daughter. I lost half of my family, she is the only one left for me."

But the girl did not agree. She was crying. The mother told her it would be ok; she should do this so that he would let them leave.

During the night, when the mother was sleeping, he brought the girl to his room and raped her. She was shouting and making noises but no one came to help her.

6

The girl cried, "You are hurting me. I am like your daughter. How can you do this to me? Please let me go." It continued like this for one week and no one was listening. The mother and daughter finally got out of the country but unfortunately, the uncle came with them.

During the journey, when he got angry, he would rape the girl, and her mother could not help her. Her body was red with blood and bruised because of physical abuse. After 7 days they came to Germany. They were in a refugee camp for one month. He couldn't disturb the girl because there were many activities for children to keep them busy and there was a committee watching the women and children.

It was time for school and they came to talk with the mother and the uncle. They said the little girl was clever and they wanted her to join the classes.

The uncle and the mother agreed. But when the workers left the uncle started shouting, "She can't go anywhere. School is only for boys, not for girls."

That night he abused her again. In the morning he told her to go and remove her name from the school list.

That day, one of the Human Rights workers sat next to the girl. She saw that the girl had bruises on her hands, on her neck and all over her body. She asked about them and the girl said she did not feel well.

They brought the girl to the doctor. The doctor did an exam and saw the truth. The little girl was so tired. She told them everything about the abuse. The workers told the girl she should go home and not tell anyone that she had told the story of her abuse to anyone.

The next day they called the girl and her mother into the office. When they told the mother that something was wrong with her daughter, she acted like she didn't know. They said, "She said that her uncle is abusing her." The mother acted shocked and said, "It is not true, he is like a father to her."
They thought the little girl had lied. Her mother took her home and beat her and told her she should never tell anyone about the abuse. But a woman from the organization that helps women and children was watching when her mother was beating her. She took the little girl away to a safe place, far away from abuse.

Story by Sisi (Bulgaria)

"My Erasmus journey was a life-time lesson for myself"

There's an old saying that says "what doesn't kill you makes you stronger", keeps me motivated to not care much about negative things. I have to think this way, as many students in Turkey also do.

An average Turkish student starts to face challenges even from primary school. The Turkish education system just cares about your grades. The system is educating us to be average people who do not question or ask why. And it was the reason why I wanted to discover other countries in order to observe if the system is also visible outside of Turkey.

At this point the Erasmus Exchange program was the best opportunity and the cheapest way to explore European countries. So, in my third year of Law School I decided to go to Poland. I had a chance to observe everything, not only the university but also about life. One year of Erasmus experience showed me some differences between my home country and Poland. Those differences have widened my perspective on life. After all, I was certain that I was missing something and I could change it.

What surprised me most about Poland? As a Law student, my answer would be about universities and the education system. While I was sharing the class with more than 400 people in Turkey; the situation was completely the opposite in Poland. You can easily guess what challenges we are going through in Turkish lecture rooms.

Aziz Emre (kneeling, left) posing for a photo with his new friends in Opole, Poland in 2018. (Photo: Aziz Emre)

Following what the lecturer says, trying to understand him/her, paying attention in the lesson is hard as hell. It is almost impossible to ask questions because it would be many people around the lecturer trying to ask questions during break.

How about in Poland? We were just 10-12 students in one class. All students were sitting around one table which makes communication easier between students to lecturer and student to student.

It was the real atmosphere for true learning. It is also about how lecturers approach students. Unlike in Turkey, there is a strong connection between students and lecturers in Polish Universities. One can easily accept that visiting a lecturer in his/her office is not a luxury, while it is a huge thing in Turkey. Getting a reply to your email in the next day is easy, while you have to wait for weeks in Turkey.

After this little comparison I have to admit that I had so many doubts about being a foreigner in a foreign country. After one year experience, I must say living in Poland was absolutely wonderful. I got the best of two worlds: Western sophistication and Eastern humility. A country firmly steeped in tradition and defined by its recent past, but secure in its future in Europe. My Erasmus journey was a life-time lesson for myself: not to fear the new, the discomfort of being in an unfamiliar place, or the dilemma of being different and needing to integrate. Seeing the world from another perspective expands your vision of how cultures can diverge on various issues and this will certainly change the way you see the future after an experience like that.

Story by Aziz Emre Yilmaz (Turkey)

Interview: "Knowledge is power"

migration_miteinander: What does education mean to you?

Sule: *Well for me it is to teach people how they can use their knowledge and how to understand others and their different perspectives and that are why I think that knowledge is power even if someone doesn't have money or political power but has knowledge. I believe this is also power to be used to change the world into something better.*

migration_miteinander: Can you talk about your experience with the education?

Sule: *I am a university student and the education system in Turkey consists of three phases: the first one is the primary school, then secondary school and high school and after that comes the university.*

But I can't talk a lot about it but I can say that my

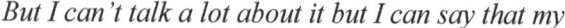

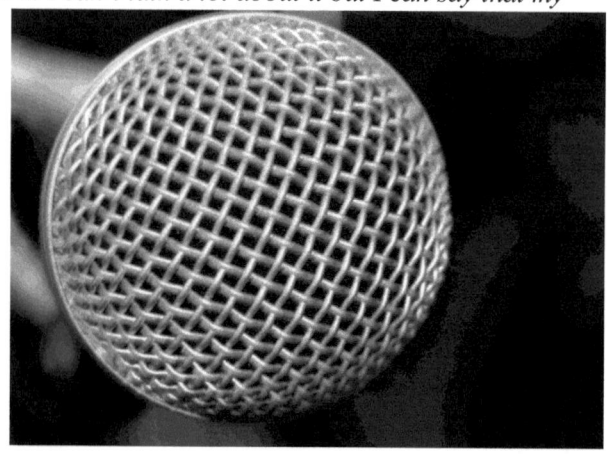

education was pretty good and funny as well and also beneficial.

migration_miteinader: Did you used to travel to other countries?

Sule: *In 2018 I was in Hungary to participate in a project that was about discrimination and hate speech. But in Turkey, I used to travel with my colleagues from the university to refugees' camps to help them to integrate in the Turkish society by teaching them some basic language skills and how to deal with daily life situations.*

migration_miteinander: Since you have been to other countries, have noticed any differences according to education?

Sule: *Actually, in Turkey we do too much in everything. Like in the school we learn a lot of things that we are not going to use in the normal life which it is different from other countries where I noticed that they concentrate on the individual skills and work on it to be developed. So, I think there is a failure in the education system in Turkey in my opinion and also the exam style is different. In Turkey school starts at the age of seven and after three years you should start doing exams but the exams in other countries are easier and more beneficial for the children in this age. Another thing is that the families in Turkey force their children to choose things they want and not things the child wants, not all the time but it is common in Turkey. Nowadays it depends more on what the person wants to study and which path the person wants to go.*

migration_miteinader: Did you choose to study business administration or you were forced to?

Sule: *Actually, it was my choice because I thought I would be beneficial for me but it was difficult because in Turkey when you study business, people would think that you will not find a job in the future and you will not be taken seriously but these things are okay. I'm used to such a thing now because I think I can work in different countries if it is hard for me to find a job in Turkey. At the end I think that the traditions and education for each country are important and should be taken seriously and in a respectful way.*

migration_miteinader: Thank you for your time.

Our interview with Sule from Turkey

Sule from Turkey (Photo: migration_miteinander)

✖

CHAPTER 2

MOBILITY

How I met the love of my life

With this short story, I want to explain to you how I met the love of my life in a foreign country. Meeting the love of my life was a journey that started many years ago and over the years I have worked very hard to reach my destination and today here I am sharing my story with the whole world. However, before meeting the love of my life I had to overcome some obstacles.

I am of the impression that travelling and living abroad as a person from a 'third world' country is one of the hardest and toughest tasks. In a world where everyone is preaching about globalization, the assertion above seems funny, but that is reality and nothing can be done to change it.

So, my story begins like this;

As a young man from Africa, I am as curious and eager to learn about my surroundings as my buddies around the world; but the only difference we have is that most of my buddies seem to have an upper hand when it comes to travelling across borders, unlike me. To travel around the world, I need a visa and getting the visa is hard as trying to buy a ticket to heaven when you are a serial sinner. My only 'sin' is being born in Africa and coming from a middle class family, without much access to the needed 'connections' to success.

After graduating from high school in Zimbabwe, a former British colony, studying abroad was a dream and I worked very hard to achieve my dream. Graduating with good grades was not much of a problem; the problem was enrolling at a foreign university in Europe, America or Asia. My dream was to study in the United

Kingdom, but one of the requirements for applying to a UK university was getting an English language certificate. Sometimes pride can kill your dreams, as someone who had used English as a language of instruction for almost 13 years at school, asking for an English language proficiency certificate was unnecessary and an absurd requirement.

The education system in Zimbabwe is like a cousin of the education system in the United Kingdom, so don't be surprised if I tell you that I actually studied William Shakespeare's literature and poetry for 2 years.

After failing to submit the required English proficiency certificate, my United Kingdom dreams disappeared into thin air, but that was not the end of my story. As someone who had also studied European history for almost 4 years, I decided to apply to a country referred to as the bridge between Europe and Asia. Yes, your guess is right; I applied to study in Turkey! And I was going to study journalism for that matter.

Getting my Turkish visa was not much of a hustle, since Turkish student visa requirements are relaxed. My journey as an international student was promising fireworks, I was prepared to face new challenges in life, explore the world and learn a new culture and language. The university I was going to study is located in Central Turkey, far away from the 'European' side of Turkey. I found myself in a very conservative city called Konya and a new episode of my life started.

Studying journalism in Turkey is a hard task given the current circumstances. The first days of my stay in Turkey were not as colorful, adapting to my situation was taking long and culture shock was directly taking its toll on me. Interacting with people around me was hard;

most of the people had little or no knowledge of English. I had to enlist the services of a translator to help me with university registration and other official documentation.

Most shops without price lists always overcharged me because of the language barrier. Luckily, my university offers exchange programs to go to 'abroad', so my dream of experiencing the real 'European' vibe was about to come true. I applied to take part in the Erasmus+ Student Exchange program. I chose Belgium as an exchange destination, the dream of living near the headquarters of the European Union was vivid in front of me. Without hesitating and wasting time, I gathered all the required documents and applied for my visa.

When I applied for my visa, I was so optimistic and I waited for the normal 15 days of processing to pass. Right on the 15th day after I lodged my application, I received an email from the Belgian Consulate in Istanbul. Well, the contents of the email were awful and I nearly lost my temper. They were notifying me that they had sent my application to Brussels for "further investigation". I had to endure another long waiting period and finally the news came. My visa application had been rejected because I didn't have sufficient funds to sponsor my stay, I didn't show enough evidence that I will return to Turkey after completing my exchange in Belgium and I didn't show any proof that I still had any family ties back in Zimbabwe. The funny part was that the letter was written in Dutch, yet I had requested to learn about the visa results in English. This experience didn't stop me from pursuing my mobility dream. After a while, I applied again for an Erasmus internship opportunity in German.

However, during the selection process, I faced some personal problems and I nearly lost my Erasmus spot. The organization I applied to, accepted me and I started my visa processes.

Reason Moses (sitting, right) posing for a photo with teammates from migration_miteinander in 2019 (Photo: migration_miteinander)

The German visa application experience was swift and straightforward; and in the specified timeframe (15 days) I got my Schengen visa and I was ready to roll.

I arrived in Germany mid-July and started my internship at migration_miteinander in Witten. No literature can describe the intercultural breeze I experienced during my internship in Germany. Before moving to Germany, I had some certain misconceptions about the place, but the warm welcome I received made me feel like a little conqueror, a little Julius Caesar.

During my stay I had the chance to listen to different stories, eat different foods, make new friends and more importantly, I also found the love of my life in Witten!

Let me share with you how I met the love of my life. The first time I met the love of my life, my head was up in smoke and the situation was so tense. It took us time to get to know each other, but after I ate different food types, met new people, travelled around the country we got to understand each other. Yes, the name of the love of my life is "Interculturalism". We are deeply in love with each other and we won't let anything destroy our love!

Story by Reason Moses Runyanga (Zimbabwe)

When the heavens stop smiling at you!

Jerome moved to Germany when he was still a young man, but now he is a father of 2.

When Jerome moved to Germany, he had huge expectations and big dreams. However, expectations from his family in Africa and his lack of a valid passport make life hard for him.

His country of origin cannot issue him a new passport, because they don't recognize him as a citizen anymore. Today, Jerome is stuck in Germany and cannot move freely because of his status. For him to go out of the country he has to ask for permission and it's hard to get that kind of document. The last time he visited his country of origin was about 8 years ago and it was hard for him to get the "travelling pass." For his safety he had to be accompanied by his wife.

"I told my wife, if you want me to come back here

again, we have to go together." His wife agreed to accompany him to Africa.

When Jerome moved to Germany, the number of migrants arriving was still low and certain laws were still relaxed. He found a job in the factories, even though the job was hard he managed to work hard and buy 2 houses over the years. However due to some complications he has lost one of the houses and is about to lose the other one.

"Look at my hands," he said, stretching out his hands, "I have worked so hard to buy those houses, but you just wake up and they tell you that there are some irregularities and they are auctioning your house." His hands show evidence of his hard work, hard and rigid. To regain control of his houses, Jerome is always fighting legal battles and they are costing him lots of money.

Jerome, a father of two daughters, said that it seems like the gods are angry at him. A few years ago he divorced from his wife and the pain of losing his children and wife is straining him every day. He is not able to see his children on a regular basis and his wife moved back to her original country of birth after they divorced. "I lost my family, and I am losing my houses, the gods seem to be angry," he said sarcastically.

With his family in Africa, Jerome is expected to work hard and make sure that he provides for them. "Look brother," he said referring to the interviewer, "I have a family in Africa and they expect money from me. I always try my best but you know they don't understand what I have to go through to get the money. They think we are living like kings and queens here," he continued.

He explained that Europe has its own problems and it's not all glitters; and sometimes you have to settle for less for you to survive and earn some money. Despite all his troubles, Jerome still aims for the best and dreams of a brighter future where he is able to travel freely. "I hope that one day I will be able to get my passport and move freely. I also pray that things in Africa change for the better so that we can all go back to our motherland," he said in his closing remarks.

Story from Jerome

Here is my story...

2 011 was the beginning of the biggest switch in my life.

To be more accurate, my life started to change since the first day of the Syrian Revolution on 15 March 2011.

My name is Kasem Abdul Razak, I am a 27 years old son of a great father and an amazing mother and a brother of 3 sisters and 4 brothers.

I am just a normal person who came from Damascus' countryside, I grew up in a very small city called Harran Ala'awameed 30 km to the east of Damascus. Like everyone else I had plans for my future such as finishing my studies, then to find a good job and to try to stabilize my life but that was the case before the year 2011, where everyone started to lose something or forced to change their lives.

In 2011, I was a student at the University of Damascus studying Archaeology. Due to the revolution and what happened at that time I wasn't able to go to university because the army had closed roads that lead to

Damascus, so I couldn't finish my studies.

2012 was the hardest year of my life because at the end of that year, my hometown was attacked by the army. They were about 4000 soldiers and lots of military equipment with the help of fighter jets and about 35 tanks. That attack was so strong and because of it the whole town was empty within few hours and since December 2012, I am a Refugee.

At that time, I had to move between many towns in Damascus' countryside trying to get safety for my family and for me. During this time, I was working in a hospital trying to help injured people as much as I could and my main task was to prepare the dead corpses to be buried. After 3 months of work at the hospital I saw and prepared more than 70 corpses. Trying to find safety, I decided with my family to leave Syria and our destination was Egypt.

Kasem during a storytelling event in Witten, Germany
(2019) (Photo: migration_miteinander)

I went to Egypt with a part of my family but we couldn't

stay there more than 5 months because my mother and one of my brothers weren't able to follow us there and decided to go back to Lebanon so that we can be together again. My first year in Lebanon was a disaster because I couldn't find any kind of work to support my family and myself. But after those dark miserable days I found a job as a youth facilitator with the organization (Save the Children). I spent almost a year working there and during that time I was able to learn lots of new things and to collect some experience. However, nothing was going the way I wanted, so I decided to travel to Europe.

At the beginning of 2015 I started to convince my family with the idea of traveling to Europe. It was a very hard task to do but eventually I did it and I got huge help from them as well. My first destination was Turkey and I spent 20 days traveling between cities in Turkey trying to find a smuggler. After that I finally found one in the city of Izmir and we arranged the travel to Greece. After spending days of walking and sleeping on the roads and taking a small nap whenever it was possible, I managed to travel to Greece on 21 August 2015 at 10 o'clock in the morning. The journey was just 50 minutes but we arrived in Greece we realized that the real journey had just begun.

That trip was 10 days long, from Greece to Macedonia then to Serbia, then to Hungary and then to Austria where I had to wait more than 12 hours to make sure that everyone in my group was safe and we then continued to Germany. On 2 September 2015, I arrived in Munich. I spent one night there and then took the bus to Berlin I had a friend there I went to his place with two other friends. When we arrived there, we cleaned ourselves and prepared the first decent meal after that huge journey we had.

On 08 September 2015 we went to the police station to ask where to go to start the asylum process. On 12 September 2015, we went to a city on the border between Germany and Poland called Eisenhüttenstadt where we spent a week in a tent and after that we were transferred to another city called Frankfurt an der Oder where we also had to spend another week.

On the 26th of September 2015 I was transferred with another friend to the last place in the asylum process. We spend almost a year in a city called Luckenwalde, 40 minutes to the south east of Berlin. That year, in Luckenwalde, was the most frustrating year for me here in Germany because I had to start everything, one more time, from zero or even less.

At that time, I wasn't able to move to another city or to work or even start learning the German language. All of that was because the government took a longtime to examine and deliver my documents back to me. In November 2016 I was ready to start a new chapter in my life after receiving my documents. At that time, I chose to move to a city called Hagen in NRW, where I had part of my family already living there.

After a long bureaucratic process, I started to feel that my life was starting to be stable because at that time I had my own flat and I started my language course and the best thing is that I have my sister and my brothers around me. This made me feel safe and know that they will be here for me at any time.

One day I was visiting my sister when I met this social worker from the social office in Hagen. She knew I was taking care of my sister and her family. We had a conversation together, it was in English, and she told me about voluntary work at the social office. My answer was "yes" without hesitation. I wanted such an opportunity in order to learn the German language as fast as possible as well to find new contacts, friends and to do something so that I can feel a bit like home.

After spending a year at the social office, I was able to collect a good amount of experience and I noticed the development in my new language skills. I wanted to practice it in a new place with new people, this led me to do a youth exchange with an organization called migration_miteinander e.V.. The project was the beginning of a new chapter in my life because I decided to stay in this path to collect more experience.

Now I'm a volunteer with migration_miteinander, I now speak and write German in a very good way and I live in a nice flat surrounded by my family and friends and I feel that my life is starting to be stable and normal.

Story by Kasem Abdul Razak, a Syrian refugee living in Germany

---

From Karachi to Witten: A dream comes true!

My name is Sikandar from Pakistan. I am 19 years old and I live Witten with my family (2brothers, 2 sisters and my mother). I'm in Germany since 2017 and during those two years I am able to get to know lots of Germans, as well as other foreigners. Currently, I'm a student an 11th grade student at the vocational college and my aim is going to university. Coming to Germany was easy for me and my family because we came here by flight. There was a person who helped us to come here. First, we took the plane from Pakistan to Turkey and from Turkey to Spain where we had to wait for at least 12 hours because there was no space for us on the plane. After that we were able to take the flight to Germany.

I had to seek refuge in Germany because I come from Karachi, a well-known international city. It was however not safe because people get robbed, killed for money and a lot of bad things happen. The government does absolutely nothing to stop these crimes. Before I left Karachi, I was getting used to that, but just before we left to come here, those bad things got higher and the situation was more dangerous than before. We then decided to leave our home and go to another safe country.

At first, I and my siblings did not want to leave but my mom told us that it was for us and for our

Sikandar (standing) participating in an awareness theatre show at the (Y)our Europe Pitch Event in Witten, Germany (2019) (Photo: migration_miteinander)

future. She reminded us that we were living in a place where you are not safe even in your own house. The situation on the streets of Karachi was terrible.

26

There are people who rob phones or anything expensive from people on the street and the way they do it is very common in Pakistan. If you are walking in a secluded place or at night, someone can approach you with a gun or any other weapon and tells you to give them all your belongings, if you react peacefully and give them whatever you have, you get to live but if you try to resist or defend yourself you might get killed.

Coming to Germany and Europe was a dream come true for me. I got to meet lovely people and got in touch with the culture of an awesome country. I get to experience, in real life, everything I saw in movies. Before coming here, I expected that Germany to be well structured and my expectations were correct. Everything from the laws and rule of law is awesome.

The diversity of cultures I am experiencing here is amazing. In Pakistan we had just our own culture, the Indian culture, but here they have diversified cultures.

I am impressed with the way people here in Germany work on their own to achieve whatever they want and this is different from Pakistan, in Pakistan you have to be connected to achieve something. I like this way of living because it has taught me to depend on myself and this is good in a way because it makes me wiser.

Ever since I came to Germany, I'm now fit more than when I was in Pakistan. I noticed something when I came here: people prefer walking and cycling than using cars. This makes me fit and healthy, before I was not able to walk for 2km but now I can walk 5 km.

In Germany, I further learned to be direct about what I want and give a try to whatever I want to achieve instead of waiting for a friend or someone with position to help me.

I feel a bit blocked by mobility rules here in Germany. Since I filed my asylum documents here in Germany and my asylum request is being handled. So, for now I'm just in Germany, I hope when I get accepted I can move freely to other European countries.

Story by Sikander (Pakistan)

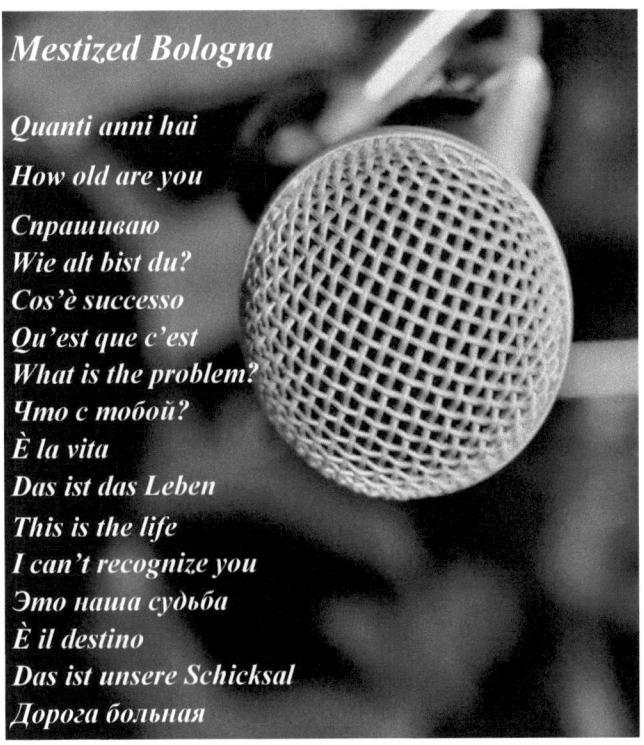

Mestized Bologna

Quanti anni hai

How old are you

Спрашиваю
Wie alt bist du?
Cos'è successo
Qu'est que c'est
What is the problem?
Что с тобой?
È la vita
Das ist das Leben
This is the life
I can't recognize you
Это наша судьба
È il destino
Das ist unsere Schicksal
Дорога больная

Si loin de notre essence
Dimmi come fai
Dimmi come fai
Don't you feel this weight?
Où allons nous
Où allons nous
Всё как раньше нужно вернуть
Ripartiamo da zero Let's try again
Troppo spesso la soffochiamo
Задыхается она
Ma tu esprimila
Nourri le fleur
Танцуй
Пой со мной
Live
Freuen sich
Pleur parfois
Ma vibra
Смейся
E vivi!

Poem by Vasily (Italy)

(Photo: migration_miteinander)

29

CHAPTER 3

IDENTITY & FAMILY

"Interracial marriages can enrich European culture"

The movement of people from one continent to another has brought with it different results and these results have created conflicts in our society. Some call it migration, and it has led some politicians and citizens to live in constant fear; it has also led some politicians to use it as a way to gain votes or popularity in their respective countries. Migration has led to intercultural marriages and the result has brought about mixed children, who sometimes end up suffering an identity crisis. These children find it hard to be accepted by both societies for example if the mother is European and the father is African, the mother's relatives can find it hard to accept them and also the African relatives can find it hard to accept a child whose mother is from a different culture and race. These children end up being caught up in difficult situations and parents are later on forced to compromise on certain issues such as religion and traditions.

Patricia (right), participating at a Youth Exchange program in Witten, Germany (Photo: migration_miteinander)

Her name is Patricia Inomwan, her father is from Nigeria and the mother is from Bulgaria. Her father moved to Bulgaria soon after the collapse of communism in Bulgaria. When her father moved to Bulgaria, things were not stable economically and politically in Bulgaria, poverty was everywhere, goods were in short supply. To buy a certain product you had to wake up early in the morning. "People were really starving, like if you want to get a bottle of milk you had to wake up at 3am, or maybe 4, to stay in the line and wait till 7 or 8 hoping that you will get it in the market, there was no supermarket, in the shop I meant to say," she explained. And now the coming in of foreigners from other parts of the world started creating problems in Bulgaria. The locals believed that the foreigners had more "privileges" than them. Everything seemed to be free and easy for the foreigners, unlike the Bulgarians who had to struggle for commodities every day.

Questions were asked whether the foreigners were there to stay or not. But in actual fact they were there for other agendas like marrying and adding value to the Bulgarian economic life. When Patricia's father met her mother, there is this question that will come in all our minds, were their parents going to accept the relationship. It was hard at first for the mother's relatives to accept a foreigner into their family.

Even though Patricia was not yet born during the time her parents met, she can testify that her father faced a certain degree of resistance because of the situation in Bulgaria was not that welcoming to foreigners. "The time that my parents met we just had the Berlin

Wall falling down and in Bulgaria we were undergoing a post communism period," she said. Between the two families, language was an obstacle. Patricia's grandparents could not speak English and her father could not speak Bulgarian; her mother acted as translator. And as we all know some facts are lost during translations. Language could not stop them from loving each other.

According to Patricia, her mother's side has a history in Bulgaria, "My mother's family come from a national hero line in Bulgaria and the family is really patriotic and they have specific expectations to certain things. They have certain values, for example as a person you should be honest, do well and always help people. These three are the core values of the family, and those values were transmitted to us," she said.

Even though her mother's family was not welcoming at first, they quickly got used to the sight of foreigners and accepted it. Having foreigners around them also gave them the opportunity of becoming 'celebrities'. Patricia's aunts became celebrities in the village where her grandparents lived since it was rare to see a foreigner in the village. "The sisters of my mum had so much fun and they were becoming popular in the village because they were the ones with the foreigners," Patricia said with a smile on her face.

Patricia was born in Nigeria and after a few weeks after her birth she was taken back to Bulgaria. That is the last time she visited Nigeria and everything she knows, thinks has its foundations in Bulgaria. Today she thinks, behaves like an "East European". The influence of her maternal family has played a major role in imparting to her Bulgarian culture, way of life, traditions and an identity. "I actually grew up in Bulgaria, so all the things that I have like mindset was formed by the things that I have seen in Bulgaria or heard from the Bulgarians, including my family. When my family moved to Sofia, my mother's family had a lot of influence on the way

Patricia (right) listening to a friend during a storytelling session in Witten, Germany (Photo: migration_miteinander)

my mother raised me up. But it wasn't in a negative way, it was just that we were taking the traditions that my mother had not

my father," she explained using a low tone and showing some signs of embarrassment. Why was she feeling embarrassed? Her father's traditions are being forgotten, her Nigerian identity is slowly vanishing, and she can't do much to repair the damage. "And here is my father... he is coming from Nigeria and he is not accustomed to certain customs. He has customs of his own dad and they don't really matter at this moment," she said. In trying to recover her father's heritage, she tries learning Nigerian Pidgin English, a form of English commonly spoken in Nigeria and has no status as an official language, but all her laboring is in vain because she doesn't understand anything and the language is too hard for her imagination. "When I was a kid, he was speaking with his Nigerian friends in Pidgin English. That was the language I didn't understand and I was really curious. I wanted to know it but I couldn't speak and I didn't know how to do it.

Like my father, I started copying it, my father is saying something and I imitate it. But you know, it was like a kid listening to a foreign song and you just repeat the words and they're actually 'nonsense'," she said.

Patricia has witnessed "clashes" between her mother and father over certain things. "For some things they (her parents) were so on a different page. I think when you're building up a family; you have to sacrifice some things. The biggest one that my mom had to compromise was baptizing us and making us Catholics," she said. Sometimes they would "clash" over the dinner menu. "They also had some things, but they were smaller like what we should have for dinner. My father almost all the time wanted to eat semolina and my mom is like 'semolina again! Let's do something Bulgarian'," she explained. Her mother was "harsh" to them as children when it comes to consuming fast food. For her mother, eating fast food is unhealthy and wrong; but her father considers eating fast food as a normal thing and something "generous" and will keep the children happy. According to Patricia, her father is opposed to eating Bulgarian traditional dishes frequently and her mother too does not enjoy eating Nigerian dishes. So because of this, the two have to meet halfway and find a compromise; the only way to solve this was making a meal with both Bulgarian and Nigerian aspects in it.

Tradition is bred in the villages so they say, Patricia got in touch with Bulgarian culture in her grandparents' village. And she is proud to say that she made her first friendships in the village. "When I think about Bulgaria, if I have to point a place where I belong, I will not point at the city (Sofia) where I basically grew up but I will say the village where my grandparents are. Because I spent my summer vacations there and for the first time I made real first friendships there and it is also the place where I fell in love with nature. This is also the time I felt a big loss. I really felt connected to this piece of land," she said. The village taught her essential life skills and gave her a way of life.

Are interracial marriages threat to European cultures and traditions? To answer this Patricia made an interesting argument, "No, European traditions can be enriched, European traditions can be made more diverse, European traditions can find more potential." In reality this is true but in the world of politics, claiming this is treasonous. European culture and traditions have diversified over the years and continue to incorporate different components from different parts of the world. In actual fact children born as a result of interracial or intercultural marriages seem to have stronger European ties. Patricia today is living a life like the rest of the East Europeans, something that was nearly impossible 2 decades ago in Bulgaria. As a person with an interracial background, Patricia believes that a person can have "a mix" of traditions and it is one of the "best things you can see in people".

Story written from an interview with Patricia Inomwan (Bulgaria)

We're just 1 in this world

We're just 1 in this world
Me and you
We and they
Whatever colour could have had your skin
For whatever reason of the meeting
And even if there would have been a clash
We remain just 1 in this world
Me against myself.

We're just 1 in this world
Universe's fuel acting in order to discover itself
Only one heart, the union within a kiss
The warm of a single being in the while of a hug
A consciousness which fills up the lights and the
shadows of the same awareness
A seed born from the same kind of love
Nurtured by the same elements
Son of the same Earth
The same sky takes care of our essence
Only one Sun and the same kind of Moon
The wheel on the season's cycle and the unique
vehicle.

We're just 1 in this world
A voice and it's choir
The nice and the ugly
The rich and the poor
The short, the tall, the ignorant, the gentle
We're the same joy at a party

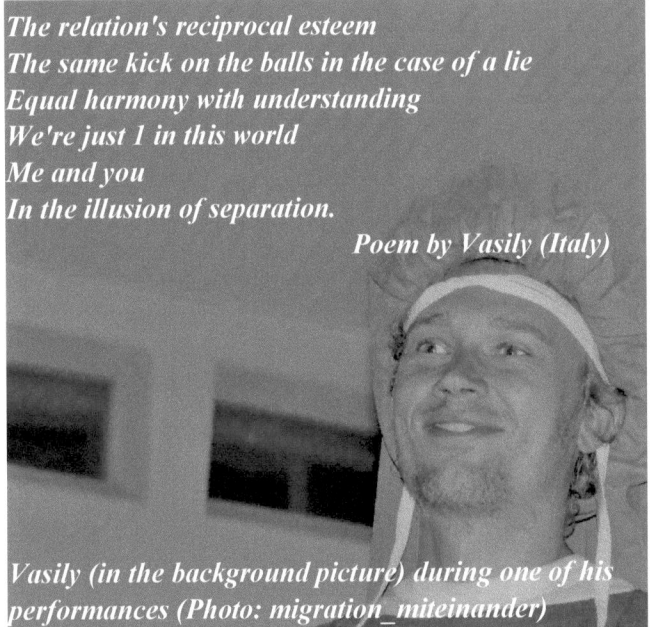

The relation's reciprocal esteem
The same kick on the balls in the case of a lie
Equal harmony with understanding
We're just 1 in this world
Me and you
In the illusion of separation.

Poem by Vasily (Italy)

Vasily (in the background picture) during one of his performances (Photo: migration_miteinander)

Bewar and his "dangerous" weapon in Europe...

W hen it comes to the usage of dangerous weapons, Europe is strict and one can get arrested, get a long jail term.

But can you imagine someone walking freely on the streets of Europe with a weapon that can shoot?

Bewar during his visit to German in 2019 (Photo: migration_miteinander)

Not all heroes wear capes they say. This man is a true hero, and he is admired by many. Some have questions though on he manages to 'escape' the long arm of the law. Here is his bitter-sweet secret and story; most stories always have sweet beginnings, but some have bitter beginnings. The ones that have bitter beginnings are always hidden and not shared. It takes courage to share a story with a bitter beginning. We don't get the chance to choose the place of our birth and this is the biggest disadvantage we have as mankind. Being born and growing up in a place where decisions on whether you should die or live are made by an 'unknown' force, can make you live a horrible life and abandon your dreams.

Being born in Iraq was not Bewar Mossa's choice, it was fate and you cannot run away from fate. But this is different from Bewar; he took a chance and ran away from his premeditated destiny. Bewar escaped from Iraq and settled in Bulgaria and he is using his camera to reveal the identity of people. Most of his subjects, share similar stories and their stories are written all over their faces. His dream of becoming a photojournalist died in Iraq. Iraq wasn't the best of options for him to start his career, but as said earlier on, we cannot choose where we want to be born.

"A picture is worth a thousand words." This is Bewar's motto and is using it a way to survive and butter his bread each morning. His lethal weapon is so unique and he uses it for a different purpose, a purpose that can change the world and make it a better place for you and me.

In a world where we struggle to understand topics like and identity and family, Bewar found an easy way to make people understand identity and he hopes that his story about his family will help you and I understand family issues.

Bewar's family is broken, not in the sense that they have family problems but 'someone' more powerful made the decision for them. Because of the war in Iraq, Bewar had to leave Iraq, some family members decided to stay and some moved to other safe places. Bewar found a safe haven in Sofia and today Bewar's family members are scattered and disjointed like a puzzle. Through the new means of communication, Bewar is able to communicate with his family and maintain strong bonds.

One of Bewar's works, titled "One shot with 10k of meanings" (Photo: Bewar Mossa)

Coming from a place where dreaming is a crime, Bewar is dreaming again and helping others dream too. He is dreaming using his weapon and attacking everyone who tries to stand in his way. Today he walks a free man in the streets of Sofia with a weapon in his hand, something he could not do in his home country.

His weapon is a Canon camera armed with a 70-300mm lense and he uses it to reflect on the different aspects of the society; sharing the emotions of people who were once not allowed to dream.

Bewar uses his camera to reproduce the aspects of identities. Most of his photographs focus on the identity of a person. To identify a person, he or she must have a face; Bewar therefore focuses on the facial impression of his subjects. His type of photography can be classified under portrait photography.

During his mobility he learned a lot about identity and decided to use the camera as a way of documenting identity, since most people these days are more interested in visuals than text. Today, Bewar is settled in Bulgaria and he is pursuing a profession in photojournalism. During his free time he does voluntary work with different non-profit organizations.

Through his photography, Bawar has managed to inspire a lot of people and help them realize their identity. The emotional expression of his subjects is captivating to the viewer. This leads to one asking questions about the pain, happiness behind the picture. For him, people are no longer interested in words but pictures.

Story written from an interview with Bewar Mossa
(Bulgaria)

Finding a family away from home

As a young lady coming from a different cultural setting, Lucia Fuentes believes in the family institution. Lucia has been to different countries, away from her family, but she has managed to remain in contact with her family and maintain strong family ties, thanks to technology.

When she was still in Peru, Lucia always wanted to study abroad and explore the world, since one of her hobbies includes meeting new people and travelling. Studying abroad offered her a chance to both travel and meet new people.

Before she moved to Germany 3 years ago, Lucia first participated in an exchange program in Spain while she was studying for her bachelor's degree back in Peru. This experience gave her the motivation and inspiration to come back to Europe and do her master's degree.

Upon completing her exchange program in Spain, Lucia went back to Peru and completed her bachelor's degree program. After completing her bachelor's degree program, she started to take German course in Lima, Peru, in preparation for yet another 'study abroad chance'. Using the contacts she had gathered during her exchange experience, she managed to move to Germany. Currently she is studying towards her master's degree.

Lucia mentoring peers at the (Y)our Europe Youth Exchange in Witten, Germany (2019) (Photo: migration_miteinander)

During her application period her parents always supported her. The major reason being that her parents didn't get the chance to study at universities and this was a great opportunity for their daughter. "Education is very important for my parents because they didn't have the chance to go to university, to be what they wanted to be in terms of studying and profession. So, for them it was very important that my brother and I study," she said.

Studying in Europe is a great opportunity for her, since she believes, Europe offers the best education and this alone was a reason for her family to feel proud. "Europe means the best quality, and German is the standard!" They say 'distance kills relationships'; this has not been the case with Lucia and her family. Though she misses her family, Lucia still maintains a strong relationship with her family back in Peru, thanks to technological advancements. "I miss my family, but thanks to technology it's possible to be in contact with my family. To write to them, to reach them, to talk, to call," she said.

Because of technology her family offers her both emotional and financial support. Lucia however feels that by not being physically present in Peru, together with her family, there are some missing links. She is not able to attend some important family events and take part in family dinners, an important aspect of the Peruvian culture. Sometimes her family hides their true emotions over the phone. In order not to worry her, her families only tells her the good parts and ignore their troubles and bad parts. "When you talk with your family, they tell you just some things, but they are not telling you troubles or they don't tell you that they are sick because they want to avoid making me feel worried."

People from the same geography tend to understand each other and have a good chance of being close to each other, this has also happened to Lucia ever since she moved to Germany. She feels connected with the people of South America and regards them as her family. They support each other and share some cultural moments together. "I feel in connection with other people who come from this big region, South America," she said, adding that she now feels more South American than Peruvian, "here I feel more South American," she said.

On another note, cultural exchanges have made her to change the way she takes some decisions, for example she can now decide to stay near a forest, close to nature, without any fear. This is something she was not able to do before moving out of Peru.

Story written from an interview with Lucia Fuentes
(Peru)

A Little Girl Abused by Her Uncle

A woman told me her sad story:
"There was a family from India that moved to Europe.
There were 5 brothers, they all got married and had families and lived together in one big house. They were happy. Their children played together and grew up together.
One of the brothers died, along with his wife. His little girl was now an orphan. Now, she lived with her eldest uncle. She was a very kind and quiet girl. All of them loved her; her cousins and her uncles loved her.

Every day she went to school with her cousin, but every day she was sleeping in class. Every day the teacher took her out of class and to the principal's office. I was working there as an accountant and every day I saw this little girl being brought to the office. Every day I tried to talk to her but she was afraid and terrified.

I tried different ways just to make her feel comfortable with me. One day, she was waiting for her driver and her cousin was not with her.

She was sitting alone in the garden of the school so I tried to talk with her again. Slowly, I sat down next to her, and asked: "How are you? How is your studying going? Why do you run away when you see me? I don't want to hurt you, I just want to be your friend." Suddenly, her driver came and she ran away without saying goodbye.

I was worried about her because of something that had happened to me in the past. And I was hoping that what I was thinking was not true. When I was a child, my uncle was abusing me and beating me. When my father and mother died, I had no one to look after me, only my uncle and my grandmother. At night my uncle would not let me sleep. When he came back from work, he would come to my room. He told me to take off my pants and put my hand inside my body. When I didn't want to do it, he would force me.

My grandmother knew everything, but she never stopped my uncle. She never told him to stop.
The cleaner in our home knew everything. They tried to help me but when my uncle found out, he killed that woman. There was no one to help me to get out of this darkness. They were afraid and did not let me go to school. So, all the time I was at home. I could only play alone or with my uncle. He was abusing me, but all the time he called this abuse "playing."

I survived this life, but now, I was afraid maybe this little girl was in the same situation. I wanted to help her. So, I started to go to their home and to teach the girl like a home teacher. First, I met the Uncle's wife. She reacted very badly; she didn't want anyone to teach the girl at home. But she could not find an excuse.

Day by day, the little girl became comfortable with me, started to talk with me. One day, she was drawing and at the same time I asked her why she couldn't sleep at night. She was drawing and talking and she told me, "At night me and my uncle are playing with each other." I was shocked because I was sure that it was the same situation that I feared. I asked her what she was playing. And why her uncle was not sleeping in his own room with these children. She said, "He is sleeping in his room but at midnight he comes to me and tells me he wants to play."

I knew she was thinking it is playing, but I knew that it was abuse. I asked her again, "What do you play with your Uncle? He is bigger than you."
She said, "When he comes, he plays with my hair. I like this because my father was doing the same and I miss him. But I don't like it when he is playing with my chest and taking off my clothes and pushing my hand inside my body. This hurts me. I don't like this. I just like when he cuddles me. I miss my father." While we were talking, her uncle was listening from behind the door. When I stopped asking questions, suddenly he entered and started shouting at me. He told me to get out. And he warned me not to tell anyone. I left but I was trying to find some other way to enter the house and find some proof. They tried to get out of the village so I couldn't find them. I informed the police but the worst thing was that they didn't listen to me because this family was the richest family in the village. They paid the police to cover their crimes.

When the police didn't help me, I went to the house to see the girl and try to rescue her from there.
I entered the house, I was calling her name but she didn't answer me.

Sisi was one of the participants of the (Y)our Europe Youth Exchange in Witten, Germany (2019) (Photo: migration_ miteinander)

When I went upstairs, she was at the window and trying to jump, to kill herself. I was trying to find a way to stop her but she wouldn't listen to me. She was shouting and telling me, "I want to die. You can't help me. They will not let me leave this house, they are bad people. They will not let you leave neither."
I couldn't stop her. When I got near her, she jumped.
We brought her to the hospital. She was in hospital for a month. They would not let me see her.
The hardest for me was that her uncle's wife knew, but she didn't stop her husband. Like my grandmother didn't stop my uncle. The day she got out of hospital, I made a

plan to escape with her. I took her. They sent the police after me, but they didn't find us. We went out of the village to the big city. I found a doctor that helped her and after 6 months she could walk again. Everything was getting better. She was happy. She was calling me mom. And to me, she was like my daughter.

We were living in the city and everything was calm. But we didn't know that this family was still following us. One day, I saw them in a park. But we hid from them and they didn't find us.

After that I was thinking of how to leave the city. If they found us they would take my daughter. I could not let that happen. One day I came home late because I was trying to get passports for us to leave the country. But the family had found my home. They took my daughter. When I arrived at home she was gone and everything was a mess. I asked the neighbors but they said they had not seen anything. I went to the police station to ask them to help me find my daughter. They started searching but then I got a phone call and they told me if I called the police, they would kill her. I said, "No, don't kill her. I will not tell the police."

But I was in the police station and they heard what I said. They made a plan to bring my daughter to me if I gave them money.

I organized this with the police. When I saw my daughter, she was crying. Her uncle had raped her and beat her, again. When I saw her, I gave him the money and he gave me my daughter. Then the police came and shouted at him, "Don't run, put down your gun." The uncle got very angry and told me, "I told you not to do this. I told you not to tell anyone. Now, I will do something that you will never forget."

He shot my daughter. This time I couldn't help her. I just lost her.
I wish she could be here with me now. But I am happy about one thing. At least she lived 6 months of her life like every single little girl, with a mother and a mother's love.

Story by Sisi (Bulgaria)

Acknowledgments

Special thanks goes to Kasem Abdul Razak who coordinated the project, guided and conducted individual interviews to collect the stories. The completion of this book could not have been accomplished without the support of Reason Moses Runyanga who took care of the final text revision and design and layout of the book. We would like to thank Griet Hellinckx who empowered the young storytellers of this book to discover their own storytelling talent, share their story and use storytelling as a powerful tool to impact our societies positively. Last but least, we would like to express our deep gratitude to each single person who contributed to the creation of this wonderful book by sharing his or her story and therewith rendering this book unique: Benjamin, Sisi, Aziz Emre, Sule, Jerome, Kasem, Reason, Sikander, Vasily, Patricia, Lucia and many more...